Japan

Your Ultimate Guide to Travel, Culture, History, Food and More!

By Asha Miyazaki

Experience Everything Travel Guide Collection™

EXPERIENCE EVERYTHING PUBLISHING

Forward

Thank you for purchasing this book from the Experience Everything Travel Guide Collection™! Inside you will find a ton of useful, informative and entertaining information on Japan and it is our desire that this book will provide you with the inspiration to explore!

Disclaimer

While this book contains a great deal of information, it does not have all of the information that is available on the Internet. It is written to inspire you about the destination rather than act as a full travel guide that you could use to get from point A to point B or to specific addresses/locations during your tour.

This document is geared towards providing exact and reliable information in regards to the topic and issue covered. The publication is sold with the idea that the publisher is not required to render accounting, officially permitted, or otherwise, qualified services. If advice is necessary, legal or professional, a practiced individual in the profession should be ordered.

- From a Declaration of Principles which was accepted and approved equally by a Committee of the American Bar Association and a Committee of Publishers and Associations:

The information provided herein is stated to be truthful and consistent, in that any liability, in terms of inattention or otherwise, by any usage or abuse of any policies, processes, or directions contained within is the solitary and utter responsibility of the recipient reader. Under no circumstances will any legal responsibility or blame be held against the publisher for any reparation, damages, or monetary loss due to the information herein, either directly or indirectly.

The information herein is offered for informational purposes solely, and is universal as so. The presentation of the information is without contract or any type of guarantee assurance.

The trademarks that are used are without any consent, and the publication of the trademark is without permission or backing by the trademark owner. All trademarks and brands within this book are for clarifying purposes only and are the owned by the owners themselves, not affiliated with this document.

CONTENTS:

Chapter I: Introduction

Japan, the land of the rising sun, is situated in East Asia. This island country is located in the Pacific Ocean. To its east is the Sea of Japan as well as the seas of South Korea, Russia and China. Meanwhile, the Sea of Okhotsk is found on the north of the island nation.

Japan holds more than 6000 islands where the four main islands of Kyushu, Hokkaido, Shikoku and Honshu comprises 97% of the country's entire land area. The capital city of Japan is Tokyo holding more than 30 million population in its greater area.

Meanwhile, the country lies east of the China Sea and the sea of Taiwan found to its south. The Japanese regime was founded along with its imperial line in 660 BC. It has been inhabited in as early as 30,000 BC. Japan also holds the longest reigning monarchy in the world. The country celebrates its foundation day every 11th of February.

Japan is surrounded by numerous mountains. In fact, more than 70% of the country is made up of mountainous terrains. There are also a lot of volcanoes found in Japan. More than 200 volcanoes are situated in the country including Mt. Fuji, which is also the tallest peak found in Japan.

The country has a fascinating culture and a rich history. Travelers find the Japanese people well organized. They are also noted for their high regard to respect and discipline.

The people of Japan are also seen to be health conscious. They limit the use of oil when cooking and prefer to eat more fish, vegetables and noodles compared to meat. If you are into eating musk melon, don't be surprised to pay as much as $300.

The healthy lifestyle of its people is probably the reason why the country has more aged population compared to anywhere else in the world. According to statistics, Japanese people live about 4 years longer compared to Americans. They can live more than 65 years, some even reach a hundred years old.

As for economic stability, Japan ranks third following the leaders US and China. The country imports about 85% coffee from Jamaica. It is also the biggest consumer of timber coming from the Amazon. Currently, there are more than 120 million people living in the country including a small number of immigrants. However, 98% of their population are ethnic Japanese.

Japan's religious sect is dominated by Buddhism with Zen Buddhism as its most common. The country's language is Japanese or Nihonggo. However, there are 4 writing systems in the country including katakana, Kanji, hiragana, romaji and katakana. Most people in Japan are able to read and write their own language but not all are able to read, speak and write English.

The national sport of the country is Sumo wrestling. You will be able to see fat, big and heavy athletes dressed in their sumo uniforms battle inside a ring. Sumo wrestlers at the Chankonabe, a kind of stew, to get really fat. Meanwhile, after the strong presence of the Americans in the country after World War II, baseball has become a popular sport in the country up to this day.

When in Japan, you don't have to worry about slurping your food inside a restaurant. This is a sign that you find the food delicious. This gesture also shows compliment to the one who prepared and cooked the meal. Japanese people also loves to eat fish. They are best known for their raw, cold cut tunas served with spicy wasabe paste. The largest fish market is also found in Japan, Tsukiji Market. It is also the country which sold the most expensive tuna, weighing 488 pounds, valued $1,735,000.

Each year, Japanese fishermen hunt whales for research purpose. However, most of whale meat end up getting sold in supermarkets. Undeniably, Japanese people eating sashimi and raw fish inside their sushi rolls. Raw horse meat has also become popular regardless of its expensive price. It is also true that the infamous Kobe beef only comes from Japan. This is because of its tight control and standards. Kobe beef can only come from the Hyogo Prefecture.

Another popular dish served in the country is the raw fugu (blowfish). Only certified chefs who passed an 11-year intensive training will be able to prepare and serve the dish. To be able to pass and get certified, you have to eat the fugu you've prepared. The trainings are crucial because fugus are dangerous and can even get you poisoned when not properly prepared.

If you are planning to visit Japan, don't be surprised to experience shakes. This is because the country experiences more than 1,500 yearly earthquakes. Most of these are minor shakes although some can be very destructive.

Japan also has a lot of customs and beliefs to follow. When meeting an older person or somebody in authority, you have to bow lower to show respect. Visiting a house will also require you to take your shoes off. Raised floors inside a Japanese household indicate that you have to take off your footwear prior entering.

Tourists who wish to enter Japan should have their currencies exchanged prior to a planned trip. This is because ATM machines don't usually accept foreign issued cards. You will have to look for a post office or a 7/11 convenient store where machines accepting foreign cards are found.

The unemployment rate in the country is only at an estimated 4%. This would mean that their people love their jobs and work hard to keep it. With their hard working and disciplined nature, the crime rate in Japan is relatively low compared to other countries in Asia. In fact, it holds the second lowest rate of homicide in the world. For every 100 people, the homicide rate is only 50. In contrast to its homicide crime rate, the country holds a number of suicide cases. It holds the extremely spooky Aokigahara forest where most Japanese commit suicide.

Meanwhile, the country is also notable for its well-organized mafia called the Yakuzas. The organization would cut off the pinky finger of their member upon incurring a first offense.

Japan's past time include watching movies and animated films. These films (anime) holds 60% of the total animation in the world shown even in TV series. The animation industry in Japan is also thriving. This paved the way for more than 100 voice-acting schools to be established to teach students the proper way of dubbing anime sounds and voices.

There are also more than 1,600 temples in Japan. Most of these are found in Kyoto and exhibit a good taste of their culture and history. If you want to be more in vogue, visiting Tokyo is a must although living in the capital city of the country can be very expensive. In fact, Tokyo ranks as the second most pricey city to live in the world. It is also a destination for most businessmen and for those who want to taste a fast paced luxurious life. If you are planning to visit the city, be sure to have a prior hotel reservation as prices can be very expensive.

The country is also known to have produced 15 Nobel prize winners. It values art, poetry, music and films. The country is also home to 3 Fields medalists and holds one winner for the Gauze Prize laureate. The Haiku is the shortest form of poetry in the world having only three lines. Takahi Miike, a prolific Japanese filmmaker, was able to make 50 films in a decade during the peak of his career.

The transportation system in Japan is convenient to use nowadays as there are already instructions written in English. You can go by plane, buses, taxis and the famous shinkansen bullet trains. These trains have been in operation since 1964 connecting passengers from Tokyo to Osaka. The first trip from Tokyo to Osaka was about 4 hours. However, nowadays you could travel the same route at 2 hours and 25 minutes, showcasing the really fast travel speed of the bullet train.

Going around the country will make you feel as comfortable as possible. You will not find it difficult to grab a meal as there are a lot of vending machines available. These machines dispenses drinks from soda, coffee, bottled water and even beer. There are also machines that dispense bento boxes (full meals in a box), noodles and sushi.

Chapter II: Japan History and Culture

The long monarchy and imperial governance in Japan is best defined by its rich history. Although the country is not as big compared to other major players in the world, Japan has taken part during a number of world wars. It has also invade some neighboring territories in the past and has launched weapons that has destroyed property and lives within and outside the country.

According to legends, the creation of Japan was made by the son goddess. This may be the reason behind the country's nickname, land of the rising sun. It was also said that the sun goddess was where the emperors of the country descended. The first emperor of the island nation was Jimmu, crowned in 660 BC.

Meanwhile, the history of the country was first recorded about AD 400. At this time, the Yamato clan started to claim authority among other clans found in western and central Japan. This was also the time when the Koreans introduced Buddhism to the country. The imperial court similar to China was first set up in the country by the Yamato clan in the 700s. However, the imperial courts did not prosper because clans wanted to overpower power each other in claim of authority.

The warrior families have also gained control and were rising to prominence. They were known as the Samurais. By 1192, the first military dictator, shogun Yoritomo from the Minamoto clan was put into power under a military government. The next 700 years were ruled by shoguns from different successors of warrior clans.

In 1542, westerners started arriving at the coast of Japan carrying Portuguese traders and missionaries. They were followed by Dutch, English and Spanish explorers who were looking to convert more people to Christianity. However, the shoguns in Tokugawa did not permit foreigners to enter their territory. It was only one Dutch trading post allowed to be set up at Nagasaki. Other attempts to reenter the country for trading did not succeed until 1853.

In 1868, the shogun regime ended and Emperor Meiji was put into power. It was also at this period that Japan returned to direct imperial rule. The country also shifted from medieval rule to a modernized power system. In 1889, a parliamentary government was formed and an imperial army was made. After which, the Japanese government started to extend their territory by invading nearby countries. Japan fought China in a nine-month war and was able to win control of Taiwan. They were also able to conquer the southern Manchuria and the Pescadores Islands.

Another war was fought by the Japanese in 1904 until 1905 against the Russians. The Japanese won the fight and claimed the southern Sakhalin. They also took the Russian's rights over the port and rail in Manchuria. The small island nation of Japan was able to seize the islands in the pacific claimed by Germany over World War I. It also leased some parts in China.

Later on, the Treaty of Versailles had Japan awarded control over these islands.

Japan later on agreed to respect the nationality integrity of China during the Washington Conference in 1921 until 1922. However, Japan invaded Manchuria in 1931 and set up a puppet state in the region called Manchukuo. This was ruled by the last emperor of the Manchu Dynasty, Henry Pu Yi followed by the invasion of China the year after.

Japan also tried to destroy the US fleet in the Pacific when they attacked Pearl Harbor on December 7, 1941. The first attack was successful gaining Japan power over a large area in the Pacific. However, the Japanese army was forced to retreat when the cities of Nagasaki and Hiroshima were bombed by US airforce in 1945. With the defeat of the Japanese imperial army, the Kuril Islands and the southern part of Sakhalin was returned to Russia while Taiwan and Manchuria was handed back to China. Meanwhile, the islands in the pacific remained under the occupancy of the United States.

By 1947, a new constitution took effect in the country making the emperor serve with ceremonial power. In 1951, a security treaty was signed between the United States and Japan. The treaty included US troops to be stationed in the country. By 1972, the country regained sovereignty. At the same time, the United States returned Okinawa and Ryuku to Japan.

After the war, Japan had to bounce back the economic scene. The country's recovery was noted remarkable after new technologies and manufacturing were done with huge success. Japan was also given large market shares in western economies. However, the economic imbalance had the United States and Japan to be in tension once again. Japan's government had close ties with its banking and industry systems. This was later on accused of protectionism. Nevertheless, it did not stop the country's growth which continued from the 1970s to the 1980s. This made the small island nation to rank the second largest economy in the world following the United States.

The postwar economic growth of Japan was deemed successful not until the 1990s. At this time, Japan's economy suffered a downturn. This was after its officials, industry leaders and bankers were confronted with great scandals. This led the country to face an economic crisis in 1998 with worse cases of recession.

The downturn in the economic condition of the country also led to the resignation of its Prime Minister Ryutaro Hashimoto in 1998 and was succeeded by Keizo Obuchi. A year after, Japan slowly moved to economic recovery. Despite is slow recovery, the country was in fear to slide back to recession which increased during the early parts of 2001.

When Prime Minister Shinzo Abe took over Junichiro Koizumi, he focused on issues regarding national concerns and hoped for Japan to influence world issues. He was also responsible in amending Japan's pacifist constitution and giving the military a prominent role in the government.

In 2006, the parliament has approved the first defense military of the country since World War II. By 2011, a magnitude 9.0 earthquake struck

Tokyo claiming more than 15,000 lives. The earthquake was then followed by a 30 ft. Tsunami which destroyed nuclear reactors in the area and killed thousands of people and damaged properties.

By 2014, the government has announced that its military will defend its allies following an approval from the Cabinet regarding the defense policy. Before, the military forces of Japan could only act if the country is put into great threat. By December of the same year, Abe was reinstated into power giving him four more years to revive the country's economy. Abe aimed to putting cash into the market and encouraged companies to create more jobs.

The Japanese culture can be seen to be strict and disciplined. Marriages were performed through Shinto Buddhist ceremonies held in hotels or banquets. Before, Japanese men and women were only allowed to be wedded to their fellow nationals. However, with the age of globalization, inter-country marriages were permitted.

The Japanese people also give respect to the elderly. They also follow customs and traditions including simple ones like "don't stick your chopsticks" on top of your rice bowl. This is a big no as it would indicate someone would soon die. Passing food using a chopstick is also prohibited as the bones of the dead is passed down from the oldest member of the family down to the youngest using a chopstick during a burial rite. Dreaming of broken plates is also a sign of a bad omen.

The Japanese people also have a classification with a small number of elites and a large number coming from the middle-class. Migrant workers and laborers are also present in the country.

Before, women in Japan are only allowed to do domestic chores. Other than that, it is the men's duty to work in the field, in different industries and the office. Women were not also allowed to take part in politics. In religion, women are still not allowed to enter certain sacred places inside the temple.

Meanwhile, the Japanese food is made up with various elements coming from different countries. Europeans, Koreans, Chinese, south and southeast Asians and those from North America have cast a great influence in Japanese food. However, traditional Japanese cuisine holds a great part in preserving cultural identity.

Japanese food is best defined with its ingredients, aesthetics and its preparation style. The staple food of the country is white rice, vitally found in every meal. Japanese food also makes use of seafood products and those coming from soy. You will find a wide selection of pickled vegetables and seafoods while in Japan. The flavors of the country's food remain simple and does not rely much on intense taste. Take note that the Japanese people has high regards to the presentation of their meal. You will find colorful dishes prepared on the dinner table along with side dishes.

Eating habits have also been reshaped following globalization. Before you will find people eating noodles noisily and sipping their soup with gusto as a sign of compliment to the chef. Now, more refined behavior of expressing a satisfied meal is observed.

Tea time is a part of the Japanese culture where proper etiquette is also observed. The manner of how you speak to the elderly and the use of grammar for polite conversations is highly regarded in the Japanese culture. Gifts, exchange of name cards and bowing is also a part of the country's culture. The Japanese also believes that you should be able to learn their language to show interest in their culture. The only foreign language allowed to be taught in schools is english. Many people find the Japanese etiquette daunting and complex. However, the Japanese people will be able to know the way of life you have been raised including your social status by the manner of how you talk and eat.

The traditional dress of Japan is called Kimono. Some people think it is an impractical and complex kind of clothing. However, it has the advantage of giving the one wearing it an elegant and graceful deportment. Nowadays, the kimono is being worn during special occasions unlike before when people in Japan use it as their every day clothes.

The nagajuban is worn underneath the kimono or the usual clothes worn today although not most Japanese are still adhering to traditional clothing.

Meanwhile, there are different accessories to be worn together with the kimono. The obiage, used to support the obi which serves as the sash for the kimono and the obijime which holds the obi. The material of a kimono is made from silk which makes is pretty expensive and elegant.

Unmarried women wear the furisode kimono while those who are already married use tomesode. Meanwhile, men's kimono are mostly black. The Montsuki is a halfcoat kimono worn with the family crest of the man. It is also worn with the hakama which is on top of the kimono. The kimono is finished by wearing an kaku-obi, made from stiff material, or the ones made from soft materials called heko-obi. Overall, the obijime plays an important role in the entire appearance of the kimono. You will be able to identify if the one wearing it is confronted with a happy or sad situation or is celebrating a special occasion.

The kimono is paired with the zori or geta footwear. It is made with wood and rice straw and has thong toes comparable to the modern flipflops. You will hear a tick-tack sound while walking every time you have these on. The Japanese culture is preserved by wearing traditional costumes during festivities.

Although western influence with regards to style and fashion have already reached Japan, the kimono, zori and geta remains to be preserved for cultural identification.

Chapter III: Modes of Transportation

Japan has a modern and convenient transportation system. It connects bigger cities to smaller areas. Tourists will no longer get lost while in the country as English signages have already been placed as translation guides to those written in Japanese. In fact, tickets have already English translations that will enable you to get to the place where you want to visit while in Japan.

The efficient transportation system of Japan is best known for its cleanliness and punctuality. A train will always arrive on time except for cases of serious emergencies. There are also a lot of people using their trains and buses. It would always be wise to purchase a ticket a day ahead of travel especially when your scheduled trip falls on the rush hour.

The four islands of the country including Kyushu, Shikoku, Honshu and Hokkaido are covered with reliable public transportation networks. Travelers can make use of these trains as they are convenient especially with the use of the Japan Rail Pass.

The majority of Japan's railway network is operated and owned by Japan Railways. Meanwhile, private companies hold the minority number of railway systems for those trips that are going in and around the metropolitan areas. Japan Railways succeeded the Japanese National

Railways after it became private in 1987 because of large amounts of debts and mismanagement.

The JR Group comprises of 6 regional railways including JR Central, JR Kyushu, JR Hokkaido, JR East, JR West and the JR Shikoku. It is also the operator of the JR Freight which operates nationwide. Meanwhile, private railway operates one line in Japan as well. This includes Tobu with operations going to the northern part of Tokyo and can take tourists to Nikko, Odakyu which operates from central Tokyo going to western Tokyo and to Kanagawa Prefecture and can take visitors to Hakone.

Tokyu, a private operator, operates in southern Tokyo taking tourists to Yokohama. Those going to Chiba from Tokyo can use the Keisei operated lines which can also take them to Narita Airport. Another private operator is Seibu which runs the suburban railway lines in the western part of central Tokyo. Meanwhile, Keikyu line joins Tokyo with southern Kanagawa and Yokohoma. Tourists can take this line going to the Haneda Airport. On the other hand, Keio line can take tourists to Takaosan while Meitetsu line operates around Nagoya and can let tourists access Inuyama and Central Japan Airport.

Kintetsu line is the biggest railway company which is privately owned. The line has operations in the south of Kinki region including Ise, Nara, Osaka, Nagoya and Kyoto. Nankai serves passengers going to the southern part of Osaka and Wakayama. Tourists can access Koyosan and Kansai Airport using this line. Osaka and Kobe are connected through Hankyu line serving the northern part of Osaka as well. Osaka is connected with Kyorto through Keihan while places in between are connected through Hanshin line. In Fukuoka, Nishitetsu operates a number of lines going around the city. Tourists can access Daizaifu using this line.

Aside from railway lines, Japan's main islands are connected to the country's capital and most major cities by high speed shinkansen. These are also known as bullet trains and are operated by Japan Railways. The bullet trains run at 320 kilometers per hour and are best known for its punctuality. You can sit on its chairs comfortably as these are spacious and forward facing. No fatal accidents have been recorded for shinkansens making it relatively safe to ride plus its efficiency to travel. Tourists can find this ride very enjoyable at the same time cost effective thanks to the Japan Rail Pass. Seat reservations can also be made at varying prices depending on the season of passengers.

Buses can also be taken when traveling within a city to another city in Japan. These buses operate in short to long distances. In big cities like Osaka and Tokyo, buses serve as the second means of transportation to railway lines. Meanwhile, cities that have less trains use buses as their primary means of transportation.

A bus ride can be intimidating to tourists because not all have English instructions. When entering a bus, you can use either the front or back door. A small machine is situated just in front of where you've just entered. You have to pickup a small paper with a number written on it. Take a look at the screen and you will find the number of the destination where you would go and the fare you have to pay in Yen. As you are nearing your destination, you have to press one button on the wall to signal the driver that you are about to go down. After reaching your destination, you have to put your ticket and the exact fare inside the box near the driver. It is always wise to bring change to save you time. If you don't have one, you can always have a changing machine to change your cash.

The Kosoku bus can also be taken for medium to long distance travel. These highway buses have overnight trips that can safely take you to a desired destination. The inexpensive fare of highway buses have caused overnight trains to slowly deteriorate operations although buses run slower than them.

You can also buy the Japan Bus Pass from Willer Express for more convenience on long distance travel. The bus pass will allow you to use it from three to five days depending on your choice. This will be valid within two months from the day of your purchase. Before, residents of the country can also purchase the bus pass. However, rules were changed allowing only tourists to make use of this convenient pass to travel. You can have this purchased online through the Willer Express website. Meanwhile, those who do not like to spend a night riding the bus can purchase the Japan Rail Pass instead although it is more expensive.

Taxis are another mode of transportation when in Japan. However, they can be pretty expensive and unnecessary especially when public transportation are more efficient and cheaper to use. However, when the buses and trains cease operations at midnight, you will have no other choice but to take a cab. Taxis are most sought after during Friday and Saturday nights.

Meanwhile, taking a cab in smaller cities like in Kyoto can be more convenient. It can also be economical especially when you travel in groups of three. Furthermore, it is a good choice for short distance travels.

Renting a car while on vacation in Japan is also a good choice especially when you have a lot of luggage brought with you or when you're traveling in groups. However, this option is only best taken when you are visiting countryside. If you are going to major cities, renting a car may not be a good choice at all. This is because public transportation in major cities are flourishing and less expensive compared to car rentals.

You have to be at least 18 years old with a driver's license to be able to drive in Japan. You should get your license converted to International Driving Permit in your homeland before visiting Japan. This will allow you to drive in the country for a period of 1 year even if your international license permits you to drive more than a year. If your country does not issue international permits, you will need to obtain a driver's license from Japan to be able to drive.

There are a number of car rental companies in Japan including Nippon Rentacar, Times Car Rental, Toyota Rentacar, Orix Rentacar, Ekiren and Nissan Rentacar. These companies operate a number of offices throughout the country. They offer cars in various sizes including buses, RVs and even large vans. You can also reserve a car for rent online as some major car rental firms have already English translations for their services. However, with the small number of car for rent services in the country, the prices may not be very competitive. Be sure to get your pocket ready for fees when you rent a car in Japan.

Ferries can also be taken when traveling domestic routes. Although most of the country's islands are connected by bridges and tunnels, smaller ones can only be accessed by means of ferries. Smaller ships also operate that takes a number of cars and people to nearby islands. Ferries are equipped with bedrooms and dormitories as well as public toilet and baths for those traveling overnight. Restaurants are also found inside ferries for quick access snacks and meals. You can book a ferry ride from terminals, online, by phone or from travel agencies. However, there are limited number of English speaking agents to assist your booking needs.

The last common form of transportation is bicycle riding. People from all walks of life are riding bicycles to access short distance destinations. You can use a bike to go to a restaurant, buy your groceries or even when you go to work. Bicycle parking areas are provided in apartment buildings and even in train stations.

The most common bicycle used in the country is the mamachari. It is built with a basket, so you can conveniently shop, and a child seat. It also has a lock and a simple lock for parking. Foldable bicycles, mountain bikes and multi-gear bikes are also available.

Tourists can rent bicycles in many places. These are convenient and cheap ways to get around the area of your chosen destination. Bicycle for rent shops are commonly found near train stations. Some of these stores require a deposit for your bicycle rental. They would also ask you to present identification cards, address and phone number of the place where you stay to ensure security.

The rental fee for bicycles vary on the number of hours you are to rent it. Usually, it costs about 100 to 300 yen per hour. Half day rentals cost 400 to 800 yen while a day's rental fee would cost about 1000 to 1200 yen. Most of these rental shops do not allow overnight rentals. However, in smaller areas where cycling is friendly to all, accommodations may provide free bicycles while others may charge a fee.

Getting around areas in Japan is not a problem given their wide range of transportation systems. All you have to do is locate the destination of your choice and check on available public transportation to get you to nearby tourist attractions.

Chapter IV: Where to Stay While in Japan

Japan is an expensive country where the biggest cost of your trip will usually fall on accommodation. You would be surprised that a hostel room can be more expensive than five star hotel in Thailand. Nevertheless, the experience in Japan will be very rewarding that you won't look at the expense of your entire trip.

If you are on tight budget, you can always scout for cheap places for accommodations.

However, trying on traditional Japanese inn should not be missed out even if it can cost a little higher than regular accommodation. You will be able to experience spending the night using a futon for a bed inside a tatami room.

Even as prices may be expensive, take note that accommodation standards in Japan are also high. This will guarantee that you won't have a bad experience inside your hotel room. Hotel rooms are mostly air conditioned and are equipped with WiFi to get you connected online. When in Kyoto, you can book a stay with a traditional Japanese inn.

However, traditional inns don't have air conditions and internet. Nevertheless, it will allow you to experience the old way of life of the Japanese people.

You can spend a night at a hostel by making a prior booking online. Take note that this is not the cheapest accommodation you can have while in Japan contrary to popular belief.

However, facilities in a hostel are much better than getting a regular hotel. You will have a nice kitchen that can save you costs from eating in a fancy restaurant. There is also a common place where you can socialize with other guests, rent a bike, use WiFi and even do your laundry. Most of the staff can also speak English making it easier for you to ask around.

When in Hiroshima, plan a stay at K's House Hostel. It offers clean small rooms with private bathrooms. The kitchen is also clean with food stacked completely. They will provide you with a map showing different restaurants within the area. Prices vary according to rooms. For instance, dorm rooms range from 2300 yen to 3000 yen per bed. Private double rooms will cost about 5600 yen to 7000 yen with shared bathroom facilities. Meanwhile, private double suites will cost you about 7800 yen. This is recommended for those who are traveling on a budget or those who are traveling alone.

Big cities also offer great deals for accommodations. Various business hotels can be booked online prior to the selected date of travel. These rooms usually have air conditioners and internet access and are best suited for those who are on a business trip. These hotels offer guests robes, shampoos,comb and other toiletries. Private bathrooms are found in every room as well as a desk and a fridge. Online bookings will have you pay around 5600 yen to 8300 yen per night.

For basic accommodation, you can try the traditional inn, ryokan. You can also stay in a family run inn called minshuku. Ryokans can be quite expensive but offer travelers a taste of Japanese tradition and culture. You will be able to sleep in a tatami room using a foton and drink tea while seated on cushions. Bathing is done communally even in the most expensive inns. Don't worry because male and female shower rooms are separated. Meanwhile, some ryokans can provide assistance for your desired bathing time. After you are done, they will provide you with cotton kimonos called yukata.

Guests using the ryokans don't need to worry about dinner and breakfast as this usually comes with the accommodation. This is also the reason why the rate is a little expensive than usual. Meals taste great and you will get the chance to eat traditional Japanese gourmet along with a multi-course meal. Meanwhile, breakfast is also provided with miso soup, rice, pickles, vegetables and salad as well as seaweed.

The cost of a ryokan or minshuku ranges from 15,000 yen to 17,000 yen depending on the location. More luxurious ryokans can also cost more per individual. Those who are on a budget may have to think twice before going to a ryokan. However, those who want to experience traditional Japanese culture without budget concerns can spend their vacation in ryokans or minshuku.

Another interesting accommodation is by spending a night or two in a Japanese Buddhist temple. The rooms are also similar to ryokan rooms with communal bathrooms. The meals are also prepared for dinner and breakfast. The only difference is that you will get to eat vegan meals. You will also get the chance to join the monks in their meditations and chants and experience their way of life.

Temple lodges can be seen flourishing in the Koya-san and Kyoto area. Other temple villages can also be found within a few hours outside Osaka. The prices also vary depending on the location of the temple. This can start from 13,000 yen for two people including meals or as much as 23,000 yen for a couple including meals as well.

If you are in Kyoto or Tokyo area, you can also book a stay in holiday rentals although there aren't much of these across Japan. Apartments are good alternatives while in these places where hotel accommodations can be pretty expensive. This is a good choice for those traveling with their families. One night can cost about 9,000 yen for an apartment in Tokyo.

For those who are staying in cities overnight, you can also try the accommodations in love hotels. As the name suggest, these hotels are typically for couples who want to have privacy. But don't worry because the rooms are clean and not as sleazy as you thought they would be. The quality of hotels are also great for their prices. You can comfortably rest for the night while waiting for your next trip by morning.

Japan offers a wide variety of accommodation for tourists visiting the country. Those who have missed the last train ride going home can spend the night in capsule hotels. The rooms are small and are equipped with TV sets. Shared bathrooms are provided and luggages can be kept in lockers. Most capsule hotels only allow accommodation for men.

Travelers who wish to visit Japan should make a prior booking to ensure an accommodation. Hotel promos are usually found online for cheaper rates. Planning a booking ahead of the travel time will also ensure great deals. Meanwhile, travelers should be able to know the events taking place in their desired destination. This is because rates often vary depending on the festivities happening in a certain place.

Chapter V: Where to Go and What to Eat

Japan has a lot of destinations for travelers who want to spend their vacation in the country. You can start visiting Tokyo followed by Osaka and greater areas in Nagoya.

These cities can offer different attractions that will make your stay in Japan memorable.

When in Tokyo, you will be amazed of the modern living mixed with old fashion architecture found in the city. You can take a trip in the biggest fish market in the world as it is located in Tokyo. Here you will be able to find good quality fish for sale including the pricey tuna. The market opens pretty early so make sure you make a reservation at 4 in the morning as there is a first come, first serve policy.

If you happen to visit Tokyo in January, May and September, you can watch the grand tournament of sumo held in the country's National Sumo Hall. If it's not tournament season, you can always watch wrestlers train in different sumo stables.

There are also more than 100 restaurants in Tokyo to choose from. You can head to Hachibe for great Japanese cuisine and good quality of sushi and sashimi. The Tsukiji Fish Market also offers meals to hungry travelers. You will be able to eat sushi and sashimi as early as 2 in the morning.

Another famous Japanese food chain in Tokyo is the Tonkatsu Wako. You can devour a huge rice bowl paired with miso soup and tonkatsu. It is also clean, affordable and serves authentic Japanese cuisine. The Kozue at Park Hyatt is also a good restaurant for those seeking fine dining. They serve seasonal menus, offers sophisticated ambiance as well as traditional Japanese food. Nadaman in Shangri-La Hotel Tokyo also offers fine dining experience, teppanyaki and sushi counters and a private dining room for guests.

Apart from the main dish, you can also try the traditional Japanese dessert called mochi. Ginza Akebono Mochi Shop offers a variety of mochi treats for the sweet tooth.

Aside from good food, you can also head to the Meiji Shrine found in Tokyo. The shrine was built by the emperor during the 19th century to commemorates Japan's opening to westerners. Wedding ceremonies are also held her during Sunday mornings. The Yoyogi Park is also a great place to unwind after experiencing the hustle and bustle of the city. It is also the choice for club meetings, play rehearsals and practice sessions for most Japanese in Tokyo.

Take a turn and refresh your mind by heading to the Shinjuku Gyoen National Garden. An English map is available making it easier for tourists to go around the garden. You can schedule a trip from March to early April and get stunned by the beauty of blossoming cherry blossoms.

The city of Tokyo also offers great views of buildings, highways and even people walking in a fast pace. You can go up to the 52nd floor of the Mori Tower to be able to see the specular sights of Tokyo. You can also head on to the Mori Art Museum for great art exhibits display. Take a walk around Shibuya crossing and experience the fast paced life of the city. You will be able to come across students, businessmen, shoppers and fellow tourists walking fast across the road.

Remember to pass by the Ebisu neighborhood for your dinner meals. You can find establishments offering sashimi, grilled meat and other casual food served on petite plates.

Visit Smash Hits, a karaoke bar, for your night out and enjoy singing your heart out with your friends in a private room. Custom made kimonos can also be checked out in Daimaru's Kimono and Yukata.

After visiting Tokyo, head on to Osaka, the country's third most populated region. You will be able to find great places to go around, shopping areas and of course, great food worth to go bankrupt.

The most famous dish to enjoy while in Osaka is the okonomiyaki. This can be likened to a pancake or an omelet. You can choose from noodles to seafood or meat to complete the classic dish. You can also try the kitsune udon, a thick noodle soup wrapped in fried tofu. Another edible tapestry to try is the hazokushi, flattened sushi in a bamboo box. And of course, get your stomachs famished by having the Takoyaki, octopus fritters, fugu sashimi and variances of sushi.

Although Osaka holds 3 million people, the region still possess the warmth of the country. You can go around Umeda to experience Japanese nightlife. Enjoy shopping down in Namba or dine over ethnic restaurants after visiting old school sushi outlets found in alleys.

Those who want to experience history can go back in time by visiting the Hattori Ryokuchi Park. Traffic is also low in Osaka making stops easier especially when you want to pose for a photographs behind rustic barns and windmills. If you want to calm your nerves and senses, head on the central Osaka for Japanese baths over numerous spas.

Take a tour up the 40 storey Umeda Sky Building and catch a tour of its floating garden situated on the rooftop of the building.

You will also love the people in Osaka due to their friendly and funny nature. Join the locals as you shop for brands in Midosuji and Shinsaibashi. Meanwhile, Denden Town is best known for its electronics where you can choose from to bring home. Amerikamura should be your next stop for vintage clothes while shopping centers in Namba and Tennoji offer great shopping experience that is less crowded than in Tokyo.

After marveling the busy streets of Tokyo and enjoying the cosmopolitan yet country charm of Osaka, you can now visit Nagoya. You can check out the

Tokugawa Art Museum where exhibits from the 14th to 18th centuries are displayed. You can also enjoy contemporary art and music while in Nagoya. Travelers can also book a tour in the Toyota Plant to see how cars are manufactured.

Of course, your Nagoya tour would not be complete without savoring the best dish the region has to offer. You can try the Miso Katsu, made with sweet sauce, the Tebasaki, deliciously fried chicken wings and the big Ebi (shrimp/prawn) fry, although you can find fried ebis almost anywhere in Japan but not as big as the ones find in Nagoya. Indulge yourself in Uirou sweet treats paired with green tea. For dinner, don't forget to have the Hitsumabushi, marinated barbecued eel, Miso Nikomo made with boiled miso and udon. Another must have while in Nagoya is the chicken and egg rice bowl called Oyakudon. Tenmusu, shrimp riceball wrapped in seawood, is also a great alternative to onigiri.

Going around Japan will make you enjoy the lively culture, rich history, great places and tourist attractions as well as good food. Be sure to get a taste of all of these to complete your entire Japanese vacation experience.

Chapter VI: Must See Festivals and Events

Japan has four seasons, winter, spring, summer and fall. All throughout these seasons are different celebrations. Tourists who wish to travel and take part in these festivals will not be disappointed as almost every shine have their own matsuri (festival).

Most festivals are held every year to celebrate the deity of a shrine or a historical event. Some events are celebrated for a day while others are celebrated all week long. Celebrations in Japan are best held with processions. The deity of the shrine is carried all over a town while being carried in mikoshi.

Other festivals are held with decorated floats roaming around the streets while being accompanied with flute music and drum beats. Each of these matsuris are celebrated according to the town's characteristics. Some are mediative and calm while others are vibrant and lively.

From early February, travelers can visit Sapporo in Hokkaido to check on the week long celebration of the Sapporo Snow Festival. The matsuri is celebrated in Odori Park where big snow and ice sculptures are made for the festival.

Meanwhile, the Yakote Kamakura Festival is celebrated in Yakote, Akita, Japan's richest region when it comes to snow, from February 15 to 16 where snow houses are built across the city.

Visiting Nara from March 1 to 14 will enable you to experience the Omizutori. This is a religious festival wherein spectators are enthralled to see torches being burnt every night on the balcony of the Todaiji Temple. Meanwhile, Takayama Matsuri in Gifu is celebrated on April 14 to 15 followed by another celebration in October. You will be able to witness decorated floats parading in the town of Takayama during the spring season and another one by autumn.

Kyoto also celebrates the Aoi Matsuri wherein more than 500 people parade the streets while dressed in aristocratic costumes from the Heian Period. The parade starts from the Kyoto Imperial Palace going to the Kamo Shrines.

Tokyo also celebrates its festival through the Kanda Matsuri during the weekend closest to May 15 only in odd number years. The matsuri is celebrated all week long with different events across the region. The festival ends with a parade of shrines coming from local neighborhoods in the area. Still in Tokyo, the Sanja Matsuri is celebrated in Asakusa on May and is the third largest festival of the capital.

In Fukuoka, make a trip in the first week of July to be able to take part at the Hakata Gion Yamakasa. The festival is highlighted with a float festival celebrated during the early hours of daytime on July 15. Meanwhile, the Gion Matsuri in Kyoto is also celebrated in July and has been ranked among the three best celebrations in the country.

If you're heading to Osaka in July, be sure to attend the Tenjiin Matsuri where a procession is held in the streets along with the parade of boats followed by a display of colorful fireworks. By August, check out the Nebuta Matsuri in Aomori City where huge lanterns and festival floats highlight the entire celebration. You can also head to Akita City on the same month for the Kanto Matsuri where more than 200 bamboo poles with 46 lanterns are attached. These are then balanced by the members of the matsuri night procession. August is also the celebration month for the Awa Odori in Tokushima City. The festival will let you take part in traditional dancing throughout the obon season in the country.

By October, Nagasaki City celebrates Nagasaki Kunchi which features dragons themed in Chinese style and a display of floats resembling ships. In Kyoto, the Jidai Matsuri is celebrated to commemorate more than 1000 years that the region has been Japan's capital before Tokyo.

Visiting Saitama in the first week of December is the perfect time to enjoy the Chichibu Yomatsuri. You will be able to enjoy the festivities held at nighttime where huge festival floats are featured.

Japan offers tourists a wide range of festivals to choose from every season. You will find it amazing to be able to see such celebrations commemorating the rich history and culture of the country. Be sure to look around for street food kiosks to keep your stomachs filled while enjoying the views during the matsuri celebrations!

See You In Japan!

We hope you enjoyed this travel guide to Japan! After exploring all of the wonderful things Japan has to offer in this book, we hope that we have provided lots of inspiration as you plan your journey. Safe and happy travels, or as they say in Japan, "yoi ryokō o"!

Experience Everything Travel Guide Collection™